GETTING YOUR BELL RUNG

Poems by Dan Provost

Luchador Press

Big Tuna, Texas

Copyright © Dan Provost, 2025

First Edition: 1 3 5 7 9 10 8 6 4 2

ISBN: 979-8-89975-007-6

LCCN: 2025939766

Author photo: Laura Provost

Acknowledgments

My thanks to the publications where some of these works previously appeared: *A Thin Slice of Anxiety, Fixator Press, Cold Rambler, Underground Voices* and *The Crossroads.*

My thanks to my brothers and sister: Tim Provost and his wife, Heather, Judi Lamarre and her husband, Kenny, Chip Provost and his wife, Jane. The Platt family Mr. and Mrs. Platt, Rich (the road gets shorter, we get tougher ha…ha!!!!), Bunny, and Tanya. Michael and Laura Cleaves— (We miss you, Mike), and to the rest of the writers out there who keep the flame going…John Dorsey, Lester Allen, Michele McDannold, Cody Sexton—and the hundreds more I'm forgetting to mention.

A big thank you to Jason Ryberg at Spartan Press. A great writer plus a hard worker, taking the time to publish my work.

Thank you again!!!!

Table of Contents

Dedicated to the love of my life, for her courage and her tenacity, Laura Provost

An asterix next to your name.

As the afternoon brings no opportunity for comfort,

just another sob unexplained.

Did That

You think, lonely
boy, that I haven't
been there- looking
over that bridge. Water
slamming frigid rocks.
Ready to accept slammed brain
matter, broken bones and
                lost memories, a
sad soul of final hopes & dreams?

Is it you?
Is it us?

Yes, my fingers have
gripped the edge
of that wooden overpass.

Tears melting, hoping
for an answer. Peering
down toward the bending
stream of
finality.

Closing thoughts,
leaving others that
shared the ride with you.

Sure kid, I own Quadrophenia
too—Pete told me about
the stare of the kill.

You're there.

The same place.

The same exact place.

Maybe the same trip I took.

Where the tempted ignored

the sign of the cross.

Or received a damning phone call from that

girl who nixed

a love

      never to

           return.

One of many possible reasons leading you

to your infamous

leap.

Talked about among senior citizens who

cross the viaduct today and discuss that *"boy."*

Who…

Yea

Never followed the
locals spin on
living through the
Lord.

Na,
pain was spilled
often—when prayers
mixed with pimps, 3 AM
stories served as holy,
pertinent warnings, while
staggering your way home.

Forged,
usually.
Failed to find the keys
to let myself in—
The place where fable blended
w/ fury.

Tears abound when I said
no to the regulars—
Who claimed their goal
was to help me see
my plight—rise toward the
Heavens.

Sit Down

Cannot mix false with
fancy,
good with evil. The demons
play six string while the angels
sing glory be…Still, you are
surrounded by angered, white
venom—while the crucifixion of
man is held in high regard &
the dogma census is noted.

Looking for steady…Hated in the axiom.
Soon, you and I will be blinded forever, no
host to cling to—nothing to see along the fiery horizon…
Crowded souls, jailed in the realm; cannot escape,
cannot find a
peaceful end.

Odd

A box upon my head takes away all my senses...
Eliminates sight, sound, taste, & smell.
Touch is just fool's gold. A necessary jest, leading
my being into a second of calm—never lasting more
than a shot to the head.

A miner's find of mummified heroics. Sinking into a rotting
figure of skeletal remains.

Me

My mind is darkness—

I see nothing, hear nothing, crave nothing, but feel
impending death. Rarely moving from the couch, lying
& dreaming of faceless strollers on city streets...

"The signs were too far to read."
Never mind being understood.

Sold yourself in various ways,
convinced that soul would be cleansed...

That lead to becoming a star.

But, as Pink Floyd said once, *You reached
for the secret too soon,*

and the various clues on lonesome,
fixated roads.

Never provided a satisfied answer
toward disappointment
"you knew was on the horizon."

God?
He was nowhere to be
found.

Better to leave well
enough alone, thought
of as a being of effort, than a
chump of glorious reward.

Writing on the Wall

Hate is transactional
These 25 Cancer meds
that I take daily, causing
gross side effects.

Watch out for the 280 pound
fat man, whose belly hangs over
his belt line…

Looking like he's in his third trimester.
Waddling into the grocery store—noticing customers
moving out of the way, so my blubber
can maneuver down the aisle.

Reaching for the adult diapers, so my "accidents"
are not noticeable to the rest of the glorious shoppers

buying their weekly supply of cookies & crackers.

…Ready to
go home, take another prednisone,
lie down and watch some b-rated
horror movie.

Courage, Camielle

Selby, Burroughs, Acker, Beachy—all too morbid—even
    for me…
Late morning gross with repeated guts & constant anal
    sex scenes.

"Too much of anything, is too much for me," Townsend
    said in one of his sad songs once.

I guess I inherited this mantra while trying to read their
stuff…while my wife was at work and my dog was
begging for a walk. No use praying to Jesus for conceded
morality while I have these weirdoes off the shelf, open
to pages that expel tantrums of tragic hedonism…

Maybe, it's just beyond my scope.
Maybe, I just need another nap.

Rubbing my bald plate, I chuck *Boneyard* by Stephen
Beachy on the floor. A story within a story about
an Amish kid who witnessed a mass shooting in
Pennsylvania and now is into writing erotic tales about
his sister and a brilliant but horny, gay brother.

12:45 PM…The lawnmowers roar, the neighbor's dog
barks, a church bell rings in the distance.

I lie, coughing in my bed…a room full of books,
scribbled notes that barely make sense…promises never
kept, and the notion that, if I'm going to die soon—my
"mass" will not contain boring catholic hymns and stiff
Sunday prayers.

Unwanted Sentry Duty

Rarely slept during my college years.
Thought every inadequacy equaled insufficient worth
    to a life
not
worth
living.

Thought about suicide daily.
Dragged through the slime & the mud, mentally.
Could not...
Would not...
Never inspired to deep discussion with students or
Professors...

So I deemed my own existence was one of bare bones
    and football practice.
Viewed my teammates as necessary beings, lives that had
nothing to do with me beyond the hash marks and goal
posts. Coaches flailed their arms, trying to teach technique
and life lessons, hitting an antique blocking sled.

We lost more than we won—usually, attended by less than
    100 people.

After games, I would lock myself in my dorm room,
drink myself blind, and destroy most of my furniture as
some sort of belligerent, token ritual, dedicated to another
week of working my ass off.

Sweat.
Blood.
Pain...

Needing to break something that was in my control...

Barely graduating with a degree in English, I ended up
working in a school for troubled children as a Child Care
Worker...

Sleep?

Never solved that issue...

Hatred Within the Proverb

I'm the Driver:

An old town…
Vermont. Pulled
over to the side,
sandwiched between two
porched sixteen wheelers.
"Berkshire Mountain Spring
Water", sketched on the side,
that saw its better days twenty
years ago, when my muscles were
strong and my thoughts were wicked.

Anyways, these rides I take
have become fewer and fewer…
Used to drive daily to clear my
mind & try to find answers to questions that
would glow in my psyche---after witnessing a
façade in some small mining town, a man
or woman trying to bemoan a purpose.
Later years, I would thank the
sober god—after seeing drunks labor
to walk, witnessing the war to see
them struggle during a restless sleep in some
doorway: a pitiful excuse, not knowing where they
were…Or, another straggler, carrying a blanket &
      pillow—
Homeless, harried, pleading—allegiance to the drink they
took years ago…

You all know where this is going…Once, I was in the
hands of the alcohol devil…Starting out at the end of
some unnamed bar, saying to myself I'll only have one or
two today…

Ending up explaining the problems of the world to some
rummy who was drinking on my dime, listening to my
foolish lectures about morality, philosophy & standard
ways of living.

Yes, I've been there, sleeping in graveyards, city parks,
anywhere I laid my head…

I prayed for no one to forgive me.
But, by the will of something, I stopped…the hangovers
were brutal, the guilts were
worse…
I took to driving, observing, and noticing things I could
care less about while I was boozing…

Sinister cancer entered my life three years ago, now, I fight
to stay awake in the late afternoon…but that's OK…

Now I can remember what I did yesterday…I can enjoy
the love of my wife and the conversations we have…

Now---I'm not so much a sin.

Frothy Words

Forgive yourself
         & you may last until
         that last step is taken.

I've hurt people
physically & emotionally.

I end--
you end---

Forgive yourself &
you may last through
the shivers of old age--
Then, in conclusion, shadows
remind one of the pain
inflicted on others.

Part of living is being an asshole.

Dying--in the final reel,
mean
nothing.

Shapeless worlds.
Dead malls & mills,
stories of rented memoires.

Children weeping, lost within.
Adults, slowly wandering alone
with regret.

I hide within long
shadows, Plath, Berryman--
those who I beg to
converse with...

A drifter waits for the
whistle of no-shows.

Shanty Trap-3 AM movie.
Sucked.

A girl walks home late at night.

Memories of my
melancholy whores.

The Creative Mind
                    Henry Bergson

Where were you when the fire went out?

Perspective on issues to be passionate about?

The pressure on Coach Scott Frost to
win at Nebraska...

Became a scornful farewell when
he was fired.

The former QB's homecoming
was a failure.

Don't Go into the Woods--2:00 AM
Horror movie.
Can't remember what it was about.

"I don't know how to love him…"

Thank you, Judas Iscariot.

Jaco

Your last day on earth poems,
thanks Chuckles Bukowski.

I don't live today...

Hendrix--Words relevant to me...
I'm not well---

When the cracks appear
through the menace to forge normal.

Fuck the past
Fuck the past
Let me breath
Let me live
Franz Wright, help from
beyond the grave.

Design a dream,
ride a pony.
Crease the phantom.

We will fall together--
But's that's OK---

We all do...

What's the shame?

We are bound to
--the gimmick--
create the Specter.

Shamefully happy...

Dregs.

Forcing yourself
                outside into
the waning, deadly
October sun.

To walk among the
stares--puffing up insecurity with
chest out, gut sucked in and clamor
for the *real* Americans among us.

Your walk becomes internal
bedlam...
A test of another
toughness---

do you want to try?
----

nod in acknowledgement of
those toothless assholes.

Daylight dips--dark winter
will be soon upon us all.

Even the townies, with their
accepted nods, a car decipher...

somewhat lies ahead.

I love the spacious background
of a city.

A Quickie on Van Zant

Ronnie Van Zant showed flashes of genius as a writer,
unfortunately he parlayed that talent within the folds of
the southern flag—keeping his kinship with the south's
most belligerent all-star's—Strom Thurmond, George
Wallace, & Bull Conner—All members of the good old
boy, asshole party, who thought they were superior to
men whose skin was darker than theirs.

It's a shame really, & sometimes, you wonder if Ronnie
and Skynyrd were the proud rednecks when the huge
stars & bars dropped behind the band while playing one
of their staples—Sweet Home Alabama, or were they
trying to grab the mantle of a new south, within the
lyrics of the song itself:

In Birmingham, they love the governor...
Boo, Boo, Boo

Now we all did what we could do...

Possible break from Jim Crow, useless hatred,
sectionalism...racism?

To tell you the truth, I don't know. I do know his fat
little brother, Johnny—who's collecting every nickel
on the back of the original band's guts, is a Fox News
Bloodhound who loves God, guns, DeSantis, Trump,
and anything right-wing.

Anyways, a couple more things to mention then I'll get off my Ronnie rant. While many critics stereotyped Ronnie as a boogie freak who wrote about fighting in dive bars, his songs contained much more important subject matter. Many of his tunes dealt with the environment, the misuse of drugs, gun control, and he walked the line with the certainty of death. Despite all these classics, he *never wrote any of them down.* "If you have to write them down, they ain't worth remembering," he once told Bob Burns, the original drummer, who died in 2018.

Except for Artimus Pyle they are all gone…
Rest in Peace, Lynyrd Skynyrd.

Does your conscious bother you
tell the truth.

No More Bullshit

At least
the emptiness
is truthful.

As dead brain
matter continues
to converse on dead
entrance ramps—openings
to floral hospices that
enact the end as spiritual
and routine.

Still, I am gone inside.

Refusing to listen to those
who assume the final act is just
another part of life.

My silence is not vengeance,
but just another violation
of sadness—that enters
when the day refuses
to acknowledge those who
replicate living.

All that is left, is
The cleaning of grief mops.

A motion of ritual.
Prayers never answered.

The predictable
end.

Late

Did the noise from
the underground force,
those who dug Old Henry up—

wander like plagued zombies.

Looking for cocaine at 1 AM, while Jesus
muttered to himself about bringing Lazarus
back to life.

As Henry was cleaned up, quizzically staring at the
Beatniks who just wanted a taste of dirty

                                     living.

Jack gave a sign of the cross.
Neal motioned for all the bohemians to get their ass on the bus.

The Lord did one more rail, and smiled his way in…

Your Perspective

John wasn't a profit
until *Rain* poured onto
the world in 1966…

The New PR Tool

Depression, death?
Used more as a
marketing tool than
a cause for sadness.

You drank too much Vodka,
Trashing every venue you played

Your fans loved you…

Sitting alone in your roach infested room,
Writing a lonely manifesto that connects with Gen X
& their outcast condition—

Man, did they bond with you.

Jack Daniels T-shirts.
Marlborough "Reds" cigarettes.
Smoked only by cool guys and gals.

America sniffed and cried over
the 27-year-old club members…but held
you to genius status…intellectual folly,
only to be understood by hippies, goth & emo
heroes-- who gaped their being to be shadows of
your soul.

…while production
companies, pawn shops, movie theaters filming

biographies-- turned alcoholics, drug addicts, mental health gurus, playtime bizarros—into ca ching, ca ching... revenues...filling wallets with stories of death & human destruction.

Yes...fellow worshippers---you tattoo Kurt Cobain on your arm, buy Jesus Christ sunglasses, take the tour of Spahn Ranch and convince yourself that Chuck Manson really was a fine lyricist.

Above ground, relatives and hanger-on's still live off the estate of Michael Jackson.

Ca ching...ca ching...

Notebook Entry

I've never felt comfortable existing as a human being. Feeling that, while I had the ability to see, hear and walk—I lacked the capacity to comprehend what my surroundings are. There is a plane somewhere I do not know. I cannot understand what *"we"* are & *"where"* we should be as a race of human beings. We wrong each other—every day, every minute. Too simplistic a term I know, but we are really nothing. Or at least I am nothing. This *"world"* stands for what. We hate—we kill. We compete for power of nothing. Alone, we will all be, but what is being alive? A sanction of limitless traction that gives…gives way to death? I have seen what? Wounded where? Escaped with beer & weed towards a path of nothing.

We are all void of true existence.

All of us just go through the motions—we all die and what is important about that?

A manifesto of nothingness.
A human of atoms of what?

Try Not to Remember

Memories are Pretty

Really, they're not...Because memories are lies. A slip of
the brain to help you feel something nice.
And I'm feeling.
And I'm feeling.

This strain of isolation is within isolation.

Don't matter though...We are in a dire place sheltered
in a finality of reality.

And I'm feeling.
And I'm feeling.
And I'm feeling.
And I'm feeling.

Rumpus room—belted and bloodied. This is not a chain
of events but a diluted promise. I am the fat underachiever
who America hates. Someone whose mind controls his
depressive, pathetic actions. Burnt to a crisp with his
brethren. Bodies so dead they cannot be recognized...
lines, and lines and lines of
what?
Huh?

Where are you going? Oh—I'm—just—going—to rust—
today. See—you—in—the—next—world.
Nothingness? Always? Forever? Darkness just exists until

everything

around

you

falls

and

falls

and

falls

until finality is filled. You and I, even Kathy Acker,
cannot see it. Because we have no clue what will happen
next. Who cares what happens next? Just a dribble of
action that your neighbor could give a fuck about.

Two Days in May

Wednesday, May 20:

My friends discard me like used rag weed. I do not blame
them, I do not respond to them, I am sick

        inside.

Thursday, May 21:

Here I am again.

Engulfed in suffering.

Blank faces.

Blank lives.

Sick to my stomach.

Craving a beer. (Maybe 10),

and not thinking about tomorrow.

I am false.

We all are.

But, let's not get into that—shall we.

There is still Mike and Molly.

And Leaving Las Vegas is still an option,

Isn't it?

Kurt Cobain, Montague of Heck.

Tortured soul.

Kinship of pain—sensitive.

Death, always pending.

Afraid to go into dark, then not caring…Helpless Dancer.

Is it me for a Moment, line created by a forlorn Townsend.

Here we go again; Fight the urge.

Bait the trap

Sad, one liners.

Goodbye, John

Your funeral was tender…An Irish
Sing-song of tears, beer and wishes of
being in heaven a half hour before the devil
knew you were dead.

But we haven't talked in three years, a steep
decline in our friendship was evident to the mourners
when asked if I have visited you recently.

Dreams, like closeness die easy, when you take a peek in
the valley…finding few takers keeping the torch lit.

The scourge of ignoring…focus on your own interpretation
of extinction…closeness with former pals becomes just
comic as you attend
more rituals that bury former acquaintances.

Nov 6th, 2024

The world takes what it wants…
Soon, watch the good old USA fall into the hands of anarchy.

47, An American Salute

> *We suffer on, a day, a day, a day.*
> *And never again can come, like a man slapped,*
> *news like this*

-John Berryman, *"Dream songs 153"*

The tears of potential fascism are wept across
Liberal Americans who wanted to unite…while hearing
the rherotic of the orange haired fat man who called his
country a trash can, praised Hitler's generals--claimed
certain citizens in Ohio were eating cats and dogs.

The lies breezed through every rally.
Benito, smiling—looking over his shoulder in agreement.

The MAGA seven-toothed crowd, covering their ears
when CNN or CBS did a report on the bulbous slob.

"Our hero says no wrong, he is the savior, the second
    coming of Jesus."
Today, Onald Rump is the President Elect of the United
    States.

A slap in the face to our forefathers, men & woman
who fought & died for sovereignty & civil rights, soldiers
who gave their lives At Valley Forge, Gettysburg, France,
Normandy, Okinawa, the Battle of the Bulge, Korea,
Vietnam, Iraq, Afghanistan

All wars & conflicts where men & woman struggled for
our country…And one man sat on the sidelines

due to
his bones spurs.

Females, sexually assaulted, raped by the incoming
President…a convicted felon. An attack on the Capital
spurred on by the golden boy of Manhattan…soon to be
swept under the rug by the power monger who will throw
our freedoms out to the Atlantic Ocean.

Swept away, where courage, lives lost for a cause, death
by combat…will be joined by warrants, criminal charges,
tax cheating, business frauds, evil retributions… floating
in some sick game of greed, fear, and the wrong man
obtaining the title of being the most powerful being in
the world.

Yes…we must survive this fraud, this clown of dignity,
this cheap whore in a 500 suit.

He does not deserve our respect…nor the opportunity to
lead us during the next four minutes, never mind the next
four years.

This is the greatest test as a nation we have ever had.

And, it comes from within…

Our heart…
Our soul…

All who had the gumption to call
themselves
Americans.

One Last Dance in Solitary

A prison cell that contains most of
the body.

Arms can extend a bit…
Feet can move around.

But lying down is impossible.

The time has come—attempt to breathe, dance--
all that's left is
God's good will…

Goodbye.

Saddened

Despair about our plight?

Try laughing insanity.
While taking the plunge into
no man's land.

With one foot kicking the
sand on the ocean shore,

The other plunged into the frigid
water…forming a stalactite, ready to snap
under the weight of conquering armies—ready
to claim the world.

Where no purpose exist

anymore.

Then the Band Suffered

Guitar solo.
Girls laughing.
Waitress bored.
Children, locked in
the hidden room—hoping
to be rescued from a
sex ring, operating in back
of the club.

Homeless across the
street where Jesus
tried to save them.

Failing.
Organist quits.
Thomas doubts.
Guy walks into the bar
as the band ends its
last set.
Broken man?
Customer of humanity's
disgust?

Jesus died a
long time ago.

Milton, Diner's Club.

Toxic God, We can't save
millions.

We refuse to
        save one.

Not Sure

I don't know how
all these faces I see,

some focused
some fried—

Are supposed
to affect me.

They glide alone—talk to
themselves about
wars that exist inside
their head.

Years ago in Paris…

Long, oblong skulls,
coatless bodies,
rainy days on side streets where
drug attire and hustler all-stars watch
their disenfranchised magic.

One day away from a massive hangover.

Sleepy, loopy days ahead.

I'm not blind…
Only partially decapitated.

29 days sober.

My Old Self

What I wouldn't give to
have us sitting in a bar again
at 9:00 AM—Telling lies
to one another, far from
God.

The New King

The Matador kills his
favorite bull—while the
countryside peers with
anticipation.

The You Tube crowd
films the event, waiting
for the beheading of the
defeated beast.

Some geek places a thumbs
up on the social media site…
Puffs his chest out, and proclaims
himself as the king of the screen world.

Somewhere, those who take walks
in the woods to combat fears & anxieties
have slowed to a crawl…

They have aged so quickly, while the hero
is carried on the shoulders of his followers.

All events streamed on your computer.

Winner's Circle up in the North Country

These pompous
winning scabies
drive up my
ass on New Hampshire
roadways while I'm
traveling the
speed limit...

When I look in
the rear view
mirror, they all
resemble me,
peppered goatee,
white, sagging skin, 60+,
think you have the world
by the meat grinder—

On their way to the
next John Birch
society meeting...

Or the next Corn dance.

Thank God they don't think like
me.

Am I being to braggadocios of
my mental capacity?

Too critical of these Yankee Swampers,
who still brandish the Rump flag on their
dirt filled backyard?

Really?

Am I being the jerk here?

To tell you the truth.

I really don't give a fuck.

An Old, Sad Friend

Remember when you
wanted to float in your
Canoe down the Connecticut
River---

Throughout all the
New England states.

You were lonely then—shattered from
forlorn dreams & so many broken
promises, whispered by misguided
men, whose enduring chatter sent a poor
farm girl scurrying to find a *Chances Are* lovers
fantasy.

And that river still flows…from New Haven, Connecticut
all the way to Pittsburgh, New Hampshire, where Earthy
Crunchy couples take advantage of what the world gave
them.

Beauty is in its simplest form.

Nature untouched…

Water, animals, caves, a touch of spirit.

While in some obscure graveyard in some obscure town in
Southern Massachusetts—ten years have passed…
Since you have been buried.

Six feet deep.

Ambidextrous

Our use of
        silence.

Drains the upper
        half
of forced beauty.

We become aware of
shared shadows…

Darkening
hope—of
impending

oblivion.

Boisterous/meek need
not apply.

You Chose this Option

You run your hand
through stringy, greased
hair.

Boston, what a disappointment
of a city.
Same for Providence, just
another place to be anonymous—

While your being is crying for recognition.

Wanting love, but feeling so pretentious
if you tell a stranger that
you are dying.

Short friendships formed
in other nameless towns.

Trying to cover the sores and welts
that hangs off elastic skin within a
New York Knicks Salvation Army coat.

A filthy blue mess, rips that
white feathers fly out of
when walking toward the alley.

Muffle that cough, as
lifers grant a minute of civility.

Few words mumbled
about standard streets.
Violent neighborhoods…smiles
that freeze away after cordial words
pretend how selfish this new town is.

Just another look around
disappointment.

The steps on another scope
of gravel.

Nothing gained—
Nothing new
　　　here.

Get a Job

As usual, way too
early for the job appointment.

Too late to clean the spot
on my suit, hoping to impress
the hiring guru.

So, I sat in my car, watching the
streaming slaves hustle into the
office while Rage Against the
Machine blasted out of my ancient
CD player.

The lead singer wants the
world to *"Testify."*

I just need something to pay
my bills so I didn't end up in
the street.

While I continue to stare, noticing
the beautifully manicured bushes leading
to the double decker, all brick, prison
like buildings.

I'm sure everybody has their territory stalked
inside fashionable cubicles.

Family pictures, flowers, inspirational
signs & stimulating notes hanging
along the small tan walls...pushing
all employees to bang those
sales
out...

Another car pulls in, three spaces
down---woman, early thirties—dressed
like she's ready to hit the clubs...

Low cut blouse, tight pants—constructed, blond,
woven hair. A villain playing for keeps.

I hide my head in my 2008 Honda CRV, turn down
the music—

Ample, ironic lyrics being sung by De La Rocha
"Where am I
Supposed to be?"

"Not Here..."

Almost hit the girl as I pull out of my low percentage
shot—

A 62-year-old-man...
Competing for a cold calling
cheerleading telemarketing position.

0-8 Four Years in a Row (High School)

Late November New England.
Deep freeze, 4:45 PM, sun already
set as we walked back to the locker room.

Heads down, bodies ached—minds numb
from thirty mile per hour wind gusts, our helmets
locked on frigid heads, shoulder pads stiff and
stifled, hard to get off and into our lockers.

A self-indulged path to pneumonia for sophomores,
who have the inevitable task of picking up all the
blocking dummies and equipment and throwing them
into the rusted shed…God forbid they forget anything,
for it will be laps tomorrow.

Channel 4 is predicting snow.

Another year of being crushed on Friday nights…being the
poor stepchild of the Tri-Valley League, being beaten week
after week by our big brothers.

45-7, 32-0, 52-6.

Preparing to play Westwood on Friday. Another fast exit to
a weekend of doldrums. Where Saturday morning we watch
film of ourselves getting our ass kicked.
Then spending Saturday night hoping to get someone to
buy beer for our team of thirty players.

Sunday...spent in bed, dreaming of my Algebra crush and watching the Pats getting beat on NBC.

Monday? Spent in horror...Getting ready to start the famished routine again.

Where Did You Go?

The nervous tics fraught
at six-years-old, spun through
a phantom's gest, that followed me
when depression & anxiety nearly drove
my spirit to the grave.

The music I so dearly hoped would
save me near normalcy.

Never came
back home.

Today, He is Hugh Beaumont

He believed
in beauty, once.

Now—he must
decide which cross
to carry today.

His bed
    has no sheets

Television lives
out fairy tales in
the corner of the room.

Furniture, swallowed by
dust phenoms that
never bothered to
turn the channel.

A frail stage to
live on…

Yes dear,
the rain will wash
away our plans
for the day—

Stares of age
properly placed
between the drops of
denial.

You're so Smart

Knowledge used
you as
a sacrificial pawn.

An antisocial clown, a
failed experiment that
exploded into the larvae of
disgusting, look-away human
flesh eating, laughing
icons who strived on
other steps of death's
expense.

Faith in Something Bigger

Finality
starts
by
staring at the ocean.
Encompassing your world
one wave at a time.
Filling the soul with
a
thought
of something bigger
than
    you...

Quite Simply

-- When the shadows began
to creep into the city...

Situations... Names
not important.

Castles of catastrophes added.

Fate, time and
fatigue...

--are all that's left

Starting January 1st

Buying into the whole Christmas spirit *thing*
as a kid was one of the few times I lived in
some sort of angelic glory.

Then it became January 1st and my
Dad would be angry at the world again...

I remember now why happiness never
lasted long.

A Change of Pace

It was the guy coming
the other way this time

that looked
down toward the ground...

then slowly

raised his head and

met my eyes.

We both gave each other
a nod...

An acknowledgement

of daily loss.

Nothing needed to
be said...

Words would have
been so cheap during this

fifteen second meeting.

Could have been
a simple act...just

a token hello…

But we both knew
it wasn't.

The total adds
up when

You try to look
nonchalant.

Fix your coat and
submerge the inner
sadness that is a
given when you

dare walk out the door.

I turned around to say
something—he was adjusting
his hat, shrugging his shoulders,

never looked back.

Kept walking away in his
own world of self-keeping.

You think, sometimes
that this existence is heading
in only one direction…

One goal.

One worship
of want.

Both of us understood
in that moment,

We were on our own.
To view what this lifetime

really means.

Voided Attempt

Always a hand
on his lone dollar.

Road to yank
him away—to a
never world.

And it was within
those 50-cent drafts
glasses that Troy
found disconnection—from what?

A tugging on his wallet, a
discernment with morality.

A big interruption with
the champ's surroundings.

He couldn't figure out why.
Just knowing "something"
was there, lingering along the
precipice.

The infinite of empty, where every
step broke ice into stalactite brain matter.

His continued stagger into oblivion was
visited by cackles from ancient crows, who
never left the dead of winter for a summer solace.

Bursting their boisterous message from lifeless trees,
whose leaves left in early October.

Troy felt the death of the world pander to his half-sloshed
brain.
Beers and loneliness will attack a man often that way.

But this captured him in the wrong dimension—
Frighting, morbid, surreal…words that others have used
to announce an existential threat.
This didn't seem to add up, as an unusual winter black fly
landed on his face, losing
his balance as he tried to swat the bastard away.

Thawp,
missed again.

Go away, misplace bug, wrong place.

Wrong time.
No abstaining from self-absorbing.

Even nature was giving you the wrong cracks
of inner ruins.

Empirical crisis?
Ha!

Your sights of being a man are shattered…

Shattered…

Shattered...

Gutted into the noise of wilted ground.
Give your pain a name.
Give your pain a name.

Where titles leave to
die & the lonely dare not
find justice to hinder their place

anywhere.
Troy.

Why the Broom is Better than the Brevity

Truth be told,
I still would rather
have a conversation with
the guy who sweeps up
after the high school dance
then a professor who teaches
Modern American Lit II any day
of the week.

And, if this "confession" leaves
me a bit snarky or lacking
protocol to all the MFA's out there.

I still value the middle-ager who can still
bowl a 200 game, can tell me who won the
first two Super Bowls—

Then discuss Pynchon, Phillip Dick, and Ol' Jackey
Kerouac in a serious discussion...

Any takers?

RIP Danny Casolaro

These are not
individuals
caught hitching their
dreams on a far
away power
monger.

Nor will they be
dusting ancient
castles, on the
verge of toppling
over by the next gust
of giant wind.

Table talkers are
a sly bunch, speaking
only to small, trusted
groups of men who
have the gusto to
blow away anyone who
is deemed to be a threat.

That includes nosey investigative
reporters,
who get too close—asking questions
which should never be asked.

Ending up dead in a nameless motel.

A Message to You and Me

He said to them, "Follow me,
and I will make you fishers of men."

I missed his message,
to the apostles, just
as I kicked my first copy
of Paradise Lost down the road.

Chances are rare when
the splitting of brain matter
is tendered...

Then bid on by the highest
savior, ready to take you
down the road of perception.

But time for reason is short, right
or wrong is answered on a narrow path, traveled by
saints & sinners...

Looking for the truth as they near the
finality of mortal
                    life.

Beginning & End

We all have cause
to bleed a little
when the night is lonely and
the call of death is
near...
Dampen the sheets with invalid
dreams, widen the escape
hatches around the closet...
Drip...
Drip...
Drip...
Blood forming around the
toy model of R2D2 that was
glued together in third grade.
You were a virgin
toadstool then.
A face looking to be
punched by anyone in a bad mood on
the playground.

Sure, those memories will lead to
an early grave...
No one wants to be kicked around.
But you are hemorrhaging now...
Mom and dad have been buried for a long time.
"Shut up and take it," you little pussy boy...
"I'm sure they will say nice things at
your funeral."

Late Christmas Night

Faded, aged colors shadowed the
lonely streets as I walked late on
Christmas night.

The end of holiday cheer apparent.
Happiness hides again for another 364 days.

Mariah Carey records put back into
the garage…
Collecting dust—
Slowly dying—
Until next December.

My walk
is over.

The Night I Failed to Live

She sang a song
to drive my love
but
all emotions seeped out
when the bullet she shot
out of her hidden .38 crept into my
final year of isolation.

Then, the notes,
faded,
and I slowly
died along
a chained linked fence
where the circus organ used
to play the old carnival hits.

Trash to You, Trash to Me

When the words are forced.
And all that appears on the paper
is bullshit over bullshit.

Readers will know your just
trying to fill up time.

With a bit of clunky ideas, that
string into nothingness.

Don't try to fool them.
They've been around the block
once or twice themselves,
so they know when the writer is
struggling with the posey just
to finish his aching chapbook.

Adding more but contributing less.

Do yourself a favor.
Take a nap.
Draw a picture of Spiro Agnew.
Buy yourself some Goldfish.

Just stay away from the phony poems for a while.
Before frustration, then failure lead you
to the nearest trash bin.

Amen.

Walter

Never needed the cheers from the
maddening crowds who loved watching Walter scoring
touchdowns in Chicago during the 1980's.

Just to see the man play—dodging an opponent,
or running over some dweeb who though he had the
balls to take him on one-on-one was heavenly.

Payton was a legalized beast...who had a million ways to
find the end zone.

A man of great spirit and determination. Payton loved
the game because of what it
represented to each individual player.

The work to be done off-season.
The game preparation for the regular season.
The violent intensity for the playoffs...

Paying the price was not a dusted cliche to him, it was
a sacred prayer that Walter Payton lived by for a star
studded thirteen-year career.

His bust now calmy resting in the Pro Football Hall of
Fame.

Think Quick

Small talk, bullshit's tricky pal.

The Beautiful Disease

Flagships declined
as Lowell fought, ignored, then settled
to market Kerouac's bones for dollars
and cents.

All those miracle workers
floated on hard times.
Feeling the ocean for their
sexual bidding—settling
for twenty-five bucks to have
their work featured in the *Outlaw
Bible of American Poetry.*

Buddha never enlightened me, nor did
the damned in their monkey wrench
game with God, punishing the believers by stoning the village
for collecting wood for the Sabbath while trying to survive
during the Old Testament.

Tempting the new breed of poets to fall off the pier, giving
up the language of observing everyday life.
You know who you are.

So, ride that boat solo, without
the blue whale or the classic thesaurus
in dreams that tempt the language.

The belief in the walk down the avenue…
The stool at the end of the bar…

The loneliness in the one room apartment...

Where saints & sinners shove you into the corner...
& you
cry in splendid glee...

When We Met

My wife made a list of things
I have to take care of after she
dies of cancer.

Six to eight months is all she has left.

So say the doctors.

Bullshit. We'll fight this fucker, until the gods
tell us it's over////& they suck the love++++out of
our hearts
for
good...

for
eternity...

Where we'll meet again, at McGarvey's in Manchester--
& make out like we did before, listening to Stevie Ray
Vaughn, playing some Texas Flood.

On the jukebox.

Jaded. Faded

I never became
anything when poetry
lived & died, infecting
my torn Achillies heel.

Plus, the constant limp
which slowed my walk
to a boring stammer, left
me behind the saviors
of night…who laid out
the words that echoed
to standing ovations…

Me, fighting balance just
to pay respect as the bloody
observers stood in glee…accepting
the congrats from the crowd of
wounded wannabes.

Deservedly so.

And I, fighting physical pain,
writers block, being seen by few
& far between as a has been, a nobody,
who lip synched signs for the obvious.

A plain chuck sucker, with an open net.

Words—falling out of my 1997 stained, filthy, knapsack.

Getting Your Bell Rung

Rocking in the huddle, dazed—

After another head-to-head
affair with some asshole in a
different color uniform.

Concussion was a word
never used as a serious condition
in the 1980's.

Only lame, pretty boys left
the game after getting their
bell rung.

Just an extra slosh of the
brain from one side of your head
to another...

No big deal.

You still have the 4th quarter to play.

White Guy from the Sunset Limited

Yes,

that fractured, intellectual
man will throw himself
in front of a train.

Today.

His outlets for beauty
are not tangible anymore.

Distressed with mankind's
defeats at Treblinka, 9/11, &
the Rohingya genocide.

Episodes of destruction
can never be cured within
words from celebrated
novelist.

Last minutes of life
are chosen blind.

We fail to seek—so
darkness lingers.

As the body makes

deadly contact with

The

Sunset

Limited.

Dan Provost's poetry has been published both online and in print since 1993. He is the author of 17 books/ chapbooks, including *All in a Pretty Little Row*, released by Roadside Press, in November 2023. *Notes From the Other Side of the Bed* will be published by A Thin Slice of Anxiety Press in early 2025. His work has been nominated for The Best of the Net three times and has read his poetry throughout the United States. He lives in Keene, New Hampshire with his wife Laura, and dog Bella.

This project was made possible, in part, by generous
support from the Osage Arts Community.

Osage Arts Community provides temporary time, space
and support for the creation of new artistic works in a
retreat format, serving creative people of all kinds —
visual artists, composers, poets, fiction and nonfiction
writers. Located on a 152-acre farm in an isolated rural
mountainside setting in Central Missouri and bordered
by ¾ of a mile of the Gasconade River, OAC provides
residencies to those working alone, as well as welcoming
collaborative teams, offering living space and workspace
in a country environment to emerging and mid-career
artists. For more information, visit us at www.osageac.org

Osage Arts Community